IT'S
NOT
MAGIC

THE NATIONAL POETRY SERIES

The National Poetry Series was founded in 1978 to
ensure the publication of five poetry books annually
through five participating publishers. Publication is
funded annually by the Lannan Foundation, Amazon
Literary Partnership, Barnes & Noble, the Poetry
Foundation, the PG Family Foundation and the Betsy
Community Fund, Joan Bingham, Mariana Cook,
Stephen Graham, Juliet Lea Hillman Simonds, William
Kistler, Jeffrey Ravetch, Laura Baudo Sillerman, and
Margaret Thornton. For a complete listing of generous
contributors to the National Poetry Series, please visit
www.nationalpoetryseries.org.

2018 COMPETITION WINNERS

It's Not Magic by JON SANDS
Chosen by Richard Blanco for Beacon Press

Fear of Description by DANIEL POPPICK
Chosen by Brenda Shaughnessy for Penguin Books

Valuing by CHRISTOPHER KONDRICH
Chosen by Jericho Brown for University of Georgia Press

Eyes Bottle Dark with a Mouthful of Flowers
by JAKE SKEETS
Chosen by Kathy Fagan for Milkweed Editions

Nervous System by ROSALIE MOFFETT
Chosen by Monica Youn for Ecco

IT'S NOT MAGIC

Poems

Jon Sands

Beacon Press
Boston

BEACON PRESS
Boston, Massachusetts
www.beacon.org

Beacon Press books
are published under the auspices of
the Unitarian Universalist Association of Congregations.

22 21 20 19   8 7 6 5 4 3 2 1

This book is printed on acid-free paper that meets
the uncoated paper ANSI/NISO specifications for
permanence as revised in 1992.

Text design by Michael Starkman
at Wilsted & Taylor Publishing Services

for Mom & Dad

for Josh & Kathy

CONTENTS

FOREWORD

The Incredible Poet-Out-of-Thin-Air Trick

As Emily Dickenson famously wrote, "If I feel physically as if the top of my head were taken off, I know that is poetry." When I encounter poetry that enthralls me, my reaction is a bit subtler, though no less powerful. I feel as if the very essence of the poet materializes, that the poet becomes physically present. That's how I define when poetry is poetry for me. And that's precisely how I felt from the moment I began reading *It's Not Magic*, when, ironically—as if by *magic*—Jon Sands seemed to appear out of thin air in my den, sit on the couch across from me, and begin reading his poems to me out loud. I could practically hear the timbre of his voice, see the dazzle in his eyes, follow the gestures of hands conducting the rhythms of his lines.

At its best, poetry like Sands's does indeed conjure up an undeniable presence; he entrances us with imagery that seems to lift off the page and reincarnate viscerally in the room. What's more, he alters our perceptions of reality, bending time and space. As T.S. Eliot posited, he suspends our disbelief: as he magically *appears*, we magically *disappear* into an imagined world fashioned from the abracadabra of his images. But what are the secrets behind the Sands magic act; how does he make us believe in the poetry of his stories and all his emotional complexities?

The Hand of Honesty Is
Quicker Than the Eye of Artifice

Throughout every poem in his collection, Sands never compromises or betrays the authenticity and raw urgency of his experiences in order to be a *clever* poet who yields to the temptation of crafting what's become the commonplace "highbrow poem," too often overly praised these days. Unlike those who produce that ilk of poetry, Sands doesn't mask himself or his poems behind obtuse images, cryptic language, and esoteric references in order to satisfy an elite aesthetic that conveys little outside the poetic circles they intend to impress. Without a doubt, Sands stands as his own person, his own unflinching poet with the audacity, the chutzpah, the emotional honesty and verve of Whitman, Hughes, and Ginsberg, and equally with the complex tenderness and regard for accessibility of James Wright, Philip Levine, Larry Levis, and Ada Limón. He knows his audience isn't solely other poets; he appeals to the poetic sensibilities that reside within all our souls, those who—like him—have had to contend with the universal yet specific nuances of living: the constant creating and dissolving, cherishing and abhorring, lying and confessing, accepting and rejecting of who we imagine we are, who we wish to be, and, ultimately, who we truly are and may have always been.

Pulling Imaginism Out of the Hat of Realism

A poem manifests out of the coarsest reality of our lives as we attempt to decipher ourselves by investigating our memories, our experiences, our hopes and fears, past and present. In that regard, a poem begins—rightly so—as one of the most selfish and self-absorbed of human endeavors. But paradoxically, Sands—among other extraordinary poets—understands intuitively that his poems are ultimately meant to be an artistic interpretation of his life transformed through an act of imagination, which allows a more profound truth to emerge from his life's experiences, for himself and, ultimately, for the sake of his readers. As such, poetry is simultaneously also a gift—one of the most selfless and generous of human endeavors. Sands understands this contradiction. He renders poems from the most intimate details of his life, while also letting them vanish in order to reveal the universally human: our collective need to be whole, to achieve our highest selves as we travel on our journeys filled with loss and fulfillment, failure and triumph, blame and absolution. That's what phenomenal poets like Sands do; they are guides and gurus, mediums and magicians. *It's Not Magic* is an entirely magical collection of poems that awes us, lets us believe the unbelievable and see our lives not as an illusion but as pure truth.

—*Richard Blanco*

i.

Hard to believe how small I once was.
That there was another person I came out from.
That my mother carried me inside her body.
I came from something.

— ANIS MOJGANI

LOVE POEM

Can I hand you my backpack and get loose?
My toe needs to sketch a snake on the sidewalk.
You don't mind if I shimmy and talk, yeah?
Is that a basketball? Let me trade you
these tax forms for it. I know this is an odd way
to propose, but I'm just gonna dance near you.
Soon, I won't even need to write poems.
You'll just look at my face and think,
That shit was deep. I'll twinkle an eyebrow;
you'll see my grandfather alone at the kitchen table
with the game on in the living room.
Or, I'll roll up my sleeve and you'll say,
You want to drink all my what?
I'll say, *That was supposed to be
a heart metaphor, but I'm working on it!*
Let me play you a song you'll like,
not just one I can prove I know all the words to.
I know we both love a different you,
but that's just how I do polyamory.
I have a spell for this, it's called Time-Machine.
That's Latin for *I-wish-this-had-gone-differently.*
Did you just turn my arm into a pterodactyl?
Is that an amoeba in your handbag?
Did the world just flip back to song one?
I wrote this for you, it's called The Bible:
just some shit I've been thinking about.
Let's create everything else. You know

what these ancient Egyptians need? Drake.
Poof, I just invented strawberries and syrup
then manifested myself love handles.
Oh, this old thing? I call that music.
Let's dance.

DIAPHRAGM

I had to fight through a diaphragm to be here.
I'm not offended. I know a lot of problems
that later became indispensable. So if I carve
a little room on this kitchen tile to pop an ankle,
is it too much to request a curtsy? Too much
to say that we don't know how this turns out,
but if contraception were more efficient in the 1980s
you wouldn't be dancing with the man who invented
the point on the question mark? I need
all the diaphragm ghost-babies to report
to the dance floor. I have three biological
and four dozen almost-brothers; it's time
someone looked out for their interests.
Mitchell Sands, give me that spin you'd do
when the chorus kicked in! Bernard Sands,
whisper the first sound you'd let out
the day your true love wasn't coming home.
Rachel Sands is what my girl-name would have been,
which means 1982-Rach was swimming with me
tail to tail; now I'm 30 and need her secrets.
How many spirits are counting on me right now?
One made me write that, and I know
his name is Peter because he told me.
Now I burn incense in every room
because my folks used to have sex a lot.
You expect me to believe they were trying
to keep me out? You thought all these poems

were for me? Do you know how many *Mes* there are?
You're 35 with two babies, Ghost Me?
You went down in a plane over the Pacific
the night I wrote *Turbulence?* This party is packed,
and we're going to die anyway
so what's a fire code to a ghost party?
You think you can rejection letter me into submission?
That's just called time. My first word was diaphragm,
and look at us now! Pull up ten thousand chairs
and a notepad. There are 15 million rooms in Cincinnati.
After I finish this, I'll be inside all of them.

MOONS OVER MY HAMMY

is a sandwich that I know dick about. I'm not above Denny's 3:00 AM breakfast, I'm just from Cincinnati, which means if you are classically inebriated with the moon out, that is something you do at Waffle House, where the hash brown options describe my sixteen-year-old brain cells tonight at Mark Baker's dad's town house (who is gone on business), and we play Kings until seven people have chugged the equivalent of four Natural Lights, each, from a flower vase, and my parents told me, *Just no alcohol and that's final,* which is high school-speak for *cover-your-tracks,* which is impossible for a 16-year-old. I wear American Eagle everything because it's an affordable Abercrombie, in order to look like someone who has made out with more than three girls (two of whom while I was on vacation). Tonight, Alicia Westen spends an hour over my lap at Mark's dad's vomiting into a plastic garbage bag that I am holding, and each time she passes echoey loud gas, which will define her more in our minds than that her father will die of a heart attack in seventeen months. Tonight, Amy Ballard laughs the loudest, even though in two years, she will fellate three juniors in one night, and we will write it into the senior skit for our graduating class of 630, and Coach Amberry will find me the morning of the assembly, and say, *Man-to-man, to follow through with a skit like that is the kind of thing that damages someone for life,* so I smile while backing away and say, *It is out of my control.* Tonight Ox and I throw two punches that both miss, then lock ourselves in Mark's dad's bedroom to cry and say we love each other, while Mark screams and pounds the door, and people will tell that story eleven years from now. Tonight, Jay Oliver is a 16-year-old on mushrooms who doesn't need to deal drugs, wearing Ox's XXXL highlighter-orange jump-suit, being chased through Tannenger Woods by a suburban traffic cop who shatters his femur on an oak tree. And we definitely meet at Waffle House at 3:00 AM where we know Joanne the waitress by name, pool our quarters to play Meatloaf's "I Would Do Anything for Love" 36 times back-to-back on the juke box, and I fall out of my chair on purpose to laugh on the ground. I have not lost my virginity, my grandparents, or spoken a word aloud about my father falling in love with another woman. Mark Baker uses the word *gay* seventeen times, refusing to apologize. It is four AM in 1999 at Waffle House, and I am drunk enough to loudly call him a racist. I throw up in the bathroom before taking my *scattered, smothered, covered hash browns* to go, stumble the full five miles of moonlight back to my own bedroom, weeping the entire way.

POOF

Knife, my mom is here,
I have to hide you in the closet.
Closet, this is my knife, I can cosign.
My friend is waiting outside, she's

    a red car. My knife
    is hiding in the closet,
    so I'm jumping out the window.
    My final trick is to talk forever about moving.

I saved you a seat, it's velvet.
I lied, it's moss.
I lied, those are bed bugs.
But don't *worry.*

    We're all going to die anyway,
    so seize the *diem.*
    I'm just not ready yet.
    I haven't realized my children were right,

or had children. I haven't
executed a completely selfless act.
I don't even know my mother's favorite color.
I don't mean to pry everyone open, I just—

    I don't mean to climb inside your arms
    when you were just hailing a taxi.
    I don't mean to cry, I know this is a gym.
    I'm sorry, that's the chair talking.

He didn't know I would be here *all day.*
Nighttime didn't know how long
I would talk about myself.
That I would use my own story as an example

    of something good and wait for you to nod.
    Were you using that elbow?
    Because it's where my hand wants to be. Sorry,
    this is embarrassing. What's an appropriate way

to transition from talking to kissing?
It makes it easier if you stare at me.
But in an *admiring* way,
like you want to pitch a tent on the roof of my mouth.

    NowIReallyHaveToGo.
    This can't be a surprise.
    I know you want to sleep in my clothes with me
    but these are *my* clothes!

Listen, my heart stopped beating ten seconds ago,

you don't hear me complaining about it.
Just put a shirt on this chair and call it me.
I told you I was a magician.

    I can snap my fingers and be on the Uptown 4.
    I don't owe you anything but a wave.

ORIGIN STORY: 1956

in the voice of Kathy, my mom

My first day of kindergarten, standing by the door
in a hand-me-down uniform I'd wear all week.
Another newborn stuck on my mother's breast,
Mary at her side, barely one year old,
pondering how to get back there,
just like all nine of us.
There was only so much to go around.

When they pulled Mary's body from the lake,
it was hard for any of us to feel
like we had more than our own eyes.
Each path I walked had a lake in it.
Mary was buried the next morning in Fort Lee.
That night, my mother told my oldest brother,
You have to move on with your life.
But that wasn't it. It was earlier for me:

that morning in 1956, with my ill-fit uniform,
purple shoes, hard boiled eggs in a plastic bag,
the whole of New Jersey outside my door.
I said, *You're not even going to drop me off at kindergarten
on my first day?*

She didn't say, *I love you, Kathy,*
but your two younger sisters can't even walk.
She said, *Sweetheart, Grace will take you.*

I didn't fight it.
Sure as the gray clouds outside, I knew what I heard—
Sweetheart,
you're on your own.

ORIGIN STORY

after Jeffrey McDaniel and Willie Perdomo

Cincinnati, 1999

I'm from 3-ways, 4-ways, and 5-ways are how you eat chili. Good intentions and passive aggressive bedrooms. From a school bus fat kid who clowns your corduroy, mohawk, and mom at the same time. Downtown race riots that don't make morning announcements. Two housing projects make up three lunch tables, and that's it. From nobody's racist, but know how many black friends they have. I'm from cross-country and lacrosse teams, but no one (including me) can say who Audre Lorde is. I'm from *history happened yesterday, so why the fuck do we have to learn this?* I'm from dodging assistant principals strapped with 151 and three shot glasses. Student councils and prom committees. I'm from a burning cross on Fountain Square. Gas masks of weed in basements and trust funds who deal drugs to play hustler. I'm from *how does Biggie Smalls know who Obi-Wan Kenobi is?* From one tornado levels five houses and puts 2,000 students in mandatory therapy. From another unarmed man dead on Vine Street at the hands of a pensioned cop while I shotgun Natural Light in a basement. I'm from police curfews that don't reach suburbs. Cannonballs off the high dive and chicken fighting till the titties pop out. I'm from straight flush faces and fake IDs. I'm from battle rapping on basement patios. From *that's a gay backpack, and that dude's gay.* From *maybe your father leaving will bring you and me closer together.* I'm from rolling twelve deep to a fight that won't happen. A full Sprite can across a lunch table and a fight that will. I'm from *thug till I die before I pass out* on this leather couch.

HERE'S THE REAL NEWS

Brooklyn, 2012

The hurricane hits New York this weekend
two days ago an earthquake shook down Manhattan
and no one got hurt but a few people felt dirty
and if it is true that this year tucks the apocalypse
in its knapsack and if it is true that our eyes
look over our shoulders until we smack into
something big and if it is true that a human being
is alone in the universe then why do I need to wait
to start getting busy I mean no disrespect
I need someone to gift wrap the goodies
set them down then stay and I am not talking
about sex but I am not *not* talking about sex
I have kicked through enough doors to know
when I'm not doing shit and this isn't about fear
but it's not *not* about fear and this poem is going
to manifest me and I can feel that so I am writing
it fast on the Manhattan bound A-train
begging this dude in the newsy hat, mustache,
and coffee thermos to tell me to stop
so I can snatch one of his chucks and throw it
through the closing doors at High Street I am
begging my man in steel toes across the aisle
coming off the graveyard shift arms tight
crossed asleep like this is a crib to hand me
a sticky note that just says, *no,* so I can pack
it up for good and take the Midwest by storm
it doesn't always feel good to know

what you are and I am dangerous here and I am
vain today like my heartsong is on loop
through everyone's iPod buds and I am so
white like rice milk in rice pudding over a bed
of sticky rice like my ears are concrete like
my problems are on everyone's to-do list I am
running away from my bedroom because that
is where I keep me and I can't see me like this
with the suburbs on speed dial making some big
deal of every thought I can't think of this poem
like it's not me like it's not shook by a mirror
like it's not begging me to start a fight so it can
jump back into my face or leave

PALINDROME

for my Grandmother Marge

after Nate Marshall after Lisel Mueller

My family of eight drives backwards
from cemetery to service, laughing
at a joke about to be made.
We're silent, as tears fall up our cheeks,
your casket wheels from hearse to funeral home.
My father's face becomes dry when he says,
My mother took responsibility for her own happiness.
He appreciates you now more than ever again.
I walk backwards through East Harlem with my brother
as the sun sets over the East River. I unmake my bed
and crawl inside to feel at home in this city,
the way you will once you're done being taken
care of by my parents in Cincinnati:
diaper changes, sponge baths, daily visits.
One by one, I'll lose all the friends who love
what I love, then ache for a home I've not lived in,
a woman I've not loved, an Ohio I fall toward
as you fly to New York with Grandpa,
who's alive now. I can no longer speak
about my parents' separation that hasn't happened.
I stop writing, grow bold and dangerous
with an unnameable dream. I am loud,
heavy, charming, four-and-a-half-feet tall
when Ben and I arrive at LaGuardia to visit,
the only time we'll come alone.
You and Grandpa bicker the entire drive
about the bridge he's about to choose.

But for a moment he whistles, you chuckle, then sing,
you take a slow thought—how one day, long after
your own children have arrived in,
and disappeared from, New York,
you'll conjure up a pockmarked microphone,
slick piano, a too-big stage.
How people will have no choice but to fall in love
with you. Ben and I lean into each other to watch:
How you gleam like the skyline.
How we must be about to see everything
through your eyes.

EPITHALAMION

for Ben & Wendell on their wedding day

This man you've only met tonight,
who is wearing fake glasses and a black tank top
in a dive bar in Manhattan, has made you laugh
eleven times already. He is teaching you
how to download apps on your new iPhone.
He is opening one and using his fingertip
to scribble his name across the screen
so you will remember it.
You are allowing your body
to become a song that says,
Move closer.

When it first appears,
you don't know how to name love, so it is
texting you last night and again this morning.
It is losing the other numbers in your phone
until five months pass, and it is just you
and this man lying in your bed on 25th Street,
your hand slung across his chest, nearly asleep,
a James Bond movie finishing on the TV.
Just before your eyes are meant to close
his body is an electric current in tight underwear
out of bed and dancing, pirouetting,
nearly into the television, an interpretive
spy dance that is not stopping, but blossoming
to the music of the credits, and your body is now
in tears from a profound laughter. It is no longer

just a joke, no longer just a beautiful dance.
It is the truth from a body that can only occur
in a bedroom between lovers that says,
When you are happy, I am alive.
It does not matter that it will take weeks
to name the love that sits inside you
stable as a new house.

You are traveling into your past, where he
is not, but now you see him everywhere.
In the moving van at nine years old. At thirteen
in the mirror and the bottle of pills, he was there.
In the arms of the first man to hold you
and assure you were beautiful.

He is not just dancing
perfectly around your dresser and curtains
in his underwear, he is doing it
for you.

You do not need to know that love is a word
which will travel free between you like a flock
of sparrows. That you will deliver yourself to it,
across an Uptown C train, a fire pit in Boston,
the wedding aisle in a library on the west side
of Manhattan. That there are years between this day
and the day you say that no other word

can communicate what we both know.
When you say: Husband—

because my life is my own
and I wish to give it to you.
Because I wish to apologize
and to forgive, and to come home
to you each night. Husband,
because it was true in a dive bar
and in a bedroom that we share on a street
where I walk around the block
because we have just had a fight
and I am coming home to you calm.
I name you my husband to receive you.
True today, tomorrow. My husband
because I have spent my entire life
climbing toward your name.

ii.

. . . and then there's the silence that comes back, a million times bigger than me, sneaks into my bones and wails and wails and wails until I can't be quiet anymore. That's how this machine works.

—ADA LIMÓN

IF I AM ALL THAT I HAVE

Then I am made from new sneakers, which are black,
clean, and tagged with a massive white swoosh.
Which would also make me the Thursday night
I bought them, after I finished teaching poetry
at a syringe exchange on West 37th Street in a room full
of track marks, head nods, murals, and what it means
to be at the mercy of your own body in New York City.

When the workshop got to sharing our poems, Bruce said,
My friend Jon asked me to open my closets.
To dig around in my closets. Go deep in my closets.
And I didn't like my closets. So I closed them.

When I left, it was raining so hard on this shitty
14 block stretch of 8th Avenue that it looked
like Gotham City in the first Batman movie.
And I just wanted to *try on* these shoes—
because the rain was like it would never stop,
and my closets felt deep like Bruce's,
and what kind of person really wants to compare
the oceans from which we draw our remarkable sorrows?
But, the sneaker lady gave me a discount.

Which means I'm also the Thursday night two summers
ago when I told Adam I was *surprised* he wore Nikes,
because I didn't have Nikes, and not having Nikes
meant I was doing my part. Because not long before,
my friend told me this story where Jerry Quickly,
a poet, is contracted to write a poem for the new
line of Air Force Ones, and the week before,

he picks up some underground magazine to see a photo
of an eight-year-old girl handcuffed to a sewing machine.

And Jerry ends up on speakerphone with a roomful
of Nike executives, and his poem starts—
Tobacco. Cotton. 112 million / Tobacco. Cotton.
Most of them were children. / M-i-s-s-i-s-s-i-p-p-i! /
And Jerry lost the deal right there going down
with the boat he had to sail,
not the one he was contracted for.

Last month I wrote a poem for Cisco Technologies,
and I don't really know their politics,
which is the same as saying I didn't want
to know. If someone asked what my battles are,
I might not have an answer, which maybe makes
honesty my battle, which isn't the same as not
being a liar, which I have also been. And I never
knew this would be a love poem—

but I am also the Nike watch my brother Abe loved
and gave to me from his own wrist, for no other reason
than because it was sharp, wide-faced, and his,
which does make me him,
which also makes me proud,

because he is now a father,
and he is selfless, beautiful,
and gave it without thought
because he loved me.

DECODED

You \ I
take \ nurture
my \ your
bag \ blood
and \ and
pour \ fill
its \ your
contents \ emptiness
on \ from
the \ the
sidewalk \ sky

If \ When
I \ I
wear \ undress
my \ your
hoodie \ skin
it \ it
is not \ is
in \ from
danger \ safety
it \ it
is not \ is
in \ from
solidarity \ alienation
it \ it
is \ is not
showmanship \ reality

The \ A
Interviewer \ God
asked \ answered
if \ when
I \ I
studied \ neglected
how \ why
Buddy Holly \ Little Richard
disarmed \ provoked
all \ one
black \ white
audiences \ emptiness

My \ Your
primary \ final
album \ silence
in \ on
middle \ infinite
school \ repeat
was \ is
Warren G's \ Kenny G's
Regulators \ lawlessness

"If \ When
I \ you
had \ lose
a \ the
son \ moon
he'd \ it
look \ blinds
like \ unlike
Trayvon" \ anything

Our \ Your
children \ ancestors
will \ won't
be \ be
responsible \ forgiven
for \ despite
the \ any
debts \ surplus
we \ you
have not \ have
paid \ assumed
in \ from
blood \ myths

The \ A
white \ black
girl \ boy
on \ in
stage \ reality
said \ listened
she \ he
prayed \ knew
Trayvon \ Trayvon
reached \ left
for \ despite
the \ a
gun \ prayer

I KNOW THAT SILENCE WILL GREET ME . . .

. . . yet still, black bra under translucent T-shirt
like the ghost of nighttime.

. . . yet still, air asks face
to smell an urban daffodil.

. . . yet still, mom dials me twice
when she misses my call.

. . . yet still, nine pastel crayons
for my birthday:
you make kid art
as highest praise.

. . . yet still, mom's undyed hair:
grays gleam like moonlit rivers.

. . . yet still, photograph of parents at my age.
Dad says, *How did I not tell you every day*
how beautiful you were?

. . . yet still, fingertip along forearm's underside mid-sentence:
I wouldn't change that I was born.

. . . yet still, letter to Jack on my bedroom wall
before painting it green.

. . . yet still, two-year-old with my last name
makes me pretend to throw him toward a window
but to save him each time.

. . . yet still, poem shows the door, but I have to walk through.

. . . yet still, afraid to say I read her Myspace and love her
favorite movie. Six months later, she holds me
when my cousin dies and I go to the National Poetry Slam
instead of the funeral.

. . . yet still, John Starks jumps over the coffee table,
three Bulls, and the empire of Chicago.

. . . yet still, shared taxi to opposite destinations.

. . . yet still, soft poem aloud on the Q train
while the city refuses to wilt.

. . . yet still, miniature ambassadors of silence
reach for my every move—
I'm too nimble, loose, alive.

. . . yet still, my dad on a creaky porch,
way past midnight, finally telling me the story
of his father's return.

INTERNET AS A CONCEPT IS NOT INSPIRING
for Eli

But let me say this. There is a video of my brother's son—
my only nephew for just three more weeks.

He is fourteen months old and does not crawl.
Sits legs out front, palms to the floor—

uses his torso to scoot his entire body forward
(and is way faster at this than you might imagine).

Nothing in my family can resist this child. All we do
is fall apart. I'm trying to recognize not just the beauty

of the gift, but the sender. And not just the sender
but the invisible routing of the conduit—because I am not

there, but can see as if it were my kitchen. This representative
of my lineage six feet from a full length mirror in Boston.

Not only does he use solely the force in his midsection
to propel his seated body (which is wearing a vest and tie,

I have to add) toward the mirror, when he arrives,
he leans in quick—steals a kiss from his own reflection.

Then does it again, learning the world of intimacy forty-five
seconds straight, the camera fighting to not shake because

his father (who is falling in love with his son) knows
the value of a job done correctly. I can see the whole thing

because my brother can see the whole thing. My roommates
call from the next room to find out why I am screaming.

I am in Brooklyn wearing sweatpants and a black T-shirt.
I can't pack my bags and move into his closet. I am not

a card sender, but something in this moment knows nothing
can be this beautiful without also taking something away.

Being almost-there is a kind of pain.

LAST NIGHT

for A.F.

*"Hard to put a price on those ones—and there's no reason
it shouldn't happen more often. Need to hold you tight,
Jon Sands."*   —*Text message, 4:03* AM

3:52 AM
Sprawled like bubblegum on my friend's stoop. The first time
this week I have known how it feels to be awake,
to recognize the person wearing my clothes. For a moment
we are not lonely.

3:12 AM
The owner's girl bought us another round after
they pulled down the gate. We are clearly our fathers.
Not just because we are charming, stubborn, and hammered.
We strum to the tune our families have played for years.
I two-step over a crack in the sidewalk, and the laughter—
like the nighttime—is real.

1:48 AM
We take the long stretch down 4th Av. I tell my friend
the story of my father leaving. How I was a freshman,
and my whole family gathered around the table because
no one knew how I would react. How at nine years old,
my bedroom shared a wall with my parents, and I would
wake to the sound of them lost inside each other's bodies.
How at that table I learned the difference between
how it looks and how it is.

1:00 AM
I'm afraid to write anything down these days. To document
the changing wind of my life, lest it become permanent.
To miss a person I am standing beside. To love what is
absent. To settle down without a family. To have an internet
that does not tell my story correctly. And we are on
our second last call in as many bars, and I mean that
in a good way.

11:15 PM
It's last call! and the bartender is fine enough to be
an art exhibit. My friend bailed on a Brooklyn wedding
to be here. Told the bride he was leaving a day early
for Detroit. We are two crows on a branch, two grown men
shaking the distance to learn how to say what we need.
He scoops a handful of potato chips into the bowl at his side,
slides them my way. Maybe we individually consider inviting
the bartender to the next spot. Instead, we ask if she knows
where it is.

9:15 PM
I am alone in my bedroom eating sushi, trying to unlock
the secrets of a secondhand keyboard. I only know
three chords, so I just rotate the order. We were supposed
to eat dinner at 9:00. The radio silence is a thickness
I can hold. My skin feels six inches wide. How can I know
I haven't been loved right in months?

THE WOODS

February, 2001

We cram shrooms into wheat bread with the organic crunchy peanut butter my mom bought. It tastes like bird shit. 45 minutes later, five midnight-boys depart my rusted '89 Camry for Symmes Woods, which borders the old elementary school. It is frigid, and we have on multiple coats, except for Ken, who'd been overly nonchalant when we raided my parent's downstairs closet. Ice-Man and I split off to converse with the plant life. I ask a small twig how it plans to approach its imminent fall from the tree that birthed it. A frozen creek partitions the woods. Ice-Man crosses it, then founds a new continent. I follow, and we decide sadness is not allowed. We whisper tiny goodbyes to any sorrow that has plagued us in the old world. We lie in the snow, entranced by the stars. Ken appears next to us in only a flannel. I say, *Ken, this is the greatest night of my life.* He says, *We have to go. Look at Ice-Man, he's freezing to death and doesn't even know it.* I look at Ice-Man, smiling, his back crunching the snow beneath him, pupils round as dime pieces. I say, *Ken, he looks really good to me.* Ken's teeth chatter like a plastic gag set. I put my hand on his forearm, and keep it there. *Ken—are you cold?*

I'm fine! he says. *I'm just looking out for Ice-Man. He's gone. They're going to have to cut off his feet.*

I try to absorb what my wounded friend can't allow himself to articulate. But then I lie down next to Ice-Man and it feels so much better than empathy. I quiet my head against his shoulder as we watch a plane fly across the moon. Ice-Man says, *What could possibly be so bad that you would have to travel away from it at that speed?*

TO MY OHIO, A LETTER HOME

At what age will I recite the names?
Show the kids my own red hands?
Say, *You've been choosing violence*
since before you knew what it was.
I chose it for you, as it was chosen for me.
To not know the names of the dead
is, at best, to drive the getaway car.
To call the not-knowing "optimism"
      is a dagger in the palm of a killer,
a trigger on the finger of a rent-a-cop,
the shatterer of worlds.
It's a child's bullet hole.
And whether I listen or not,
      it calls my name.

HOW I REMEMBER IT

April, 1999

Second period Geometry, Angela Fry asks me about an English presentation due sixth period worth 25 percent of my grade, and zero percent even started. I begin by closing my eyes slightly. I do everything I would normally do, just noticeably slower, until Mr. Boyle, my teacher, has to ask if something is wrong. I say, *No, Mr. Boyle. Not yet.* By American History I walk with a new hunch in my back. I slowly run into a desk, then a person. My frown like an upside-down whatever. By Physics, Zack Price is carrying my backpack. I tell my teacher, Mrs. Parrot, that *my stomach is troubled*, that if I sprint from class unexpectedly, *it's no disrespect. But I'm going to try to rough it, Mrs. Parrot*, I say. *I didn't become Secretary of the Student Council by not roughing it.*

Twenty minutes later, cheeks puffed, I break for the hallway, smack the bathroom door with both hands. No one is inside, but still I rush for the stall. The miniature tiles leave lines on my knees. My mouth is open as my body attempts to throw up anything. I make throaty noises, spitting into my own reflection in the water. The nurse will be a sympathetic pushover. My mom is at work until six, so our neighbor will have to pick me up from the office and assist me out to her minivan just as my English teacher, Mrs. May, calls up the first presentation. Mrs. May is the only person who will not believe me. Her hands cast a choleric spell as she tells me, *You can't just charm and squeak your way through life.*

But there I am: indignant and righteous. In tears, I storm from her classroom, clutching a bright yellow pass that reads *Excused Absence*, committed to the work I have done, full of wrath that anyone could look at me and see—a liar.

YOU KNOW HOW YOU TRY TO SAY A THING

and think *how* you're going to say it,
and *what* you're saying, all in one moment?

You know how you'll be sad, and just accidentally
try to make everyone sad, and once they get sad too, or don't,
it doesn't change anything?

You know how you want to make this complicated
so you can think more?

It's a real thing, to love.

You know how you build bomb shelters
just to hide when the going gets medium?
Bombs love that.

You know how you think you're vulnerable,
but you're just sharing too much?

You know how you don't say how you feel
in order to look complete,
and instead you're invisible?

CHECK OUT

Gone at the drop of

                          a text message:

a date request

                  my future in the form of a question—

days later

              an opportunity to not die, or at least not live

with the moment gone

                with silence's cape blown out behind me.

I talk to walls

               I ask myself questions and write answers

with a bright thick paint

                  until I am an incomplete world

saved in an email

                        without a door

in draft form.

              All the grace I keep to myself diminishes me

I tell a room of 60 that I am

              afraid to transform the people I love into

many strangers, how my heart
                                    walls, but this time I

took a vacation
                          made extra space to inhale

and woke up
                    turned into her arm, soft across my back

at the bottom of
                                a good morning,

the ocean.
          I laughed at what a hard, pointless rock I'd been—

I called it noble
                              but the page flipped—

to not burden
                              I didn't say anything,

the ones I love
        couldn't tell the difference between hello and goodbye

with my love.

WHO HERE IS NOT A LIAR?

Who's down to have even one silver-tongued bird tell you
who you really are? what your embrace actually means?
how each footprint you leave is a manifestation of your own
fear? Who are you ready to tell that they're not justified
in grabbing the back of your head with a shovel
for something you did? or thought? Name one person here
who hasn't let someone all the way down. Concrete down.
Graveyard down. Tell me who you are, like you're not
some Facebook saint with all the bodies stashed
in your keyboard. What imprint of an actual soul
on the bottom of your foot? You tell me one apple you left
to sway on Eden's tree. How much decorated loneliness
have you named love? How many arms have you drawn
from your own wreckage to reach into this silent midnight?
Your whole life is rhetorical. Show me whose favorite song
isn't the sound of their own noise. Give me this saint.
Show me the treasure on your insides. I've been waiting
to meet you. I've got love for you, motherfucker.
Where you at, motherfucker? The only thing I see is flesh.
The break of a fist over this wicker box of expectation.
Who here's ready to point fingers at their own solar plexus?
Where are you—you perfect shaman of love?
you rugged book-by-its-cover? Show me gold
one time, then every time. Please.

BREAK

Break me over coals that sizzle
and spice out, laid by those who
speak no better language than pain.
Break me on a long night when
I've exhausted the picture of myself
I've painted—painstakingly.
Break the me I am not. Break me
when I am slurped along sticky tile
in a messy house. Break me when
I believe I built the house and am
the house. Watch me writhe along
the plaster. Break me over something
small, love. Break love, and shove
my face into the shards. Find me
where there isn't a light for miles,
look at me, hands in my pockets
like I'm asking for it. Break me
like it's the only truth I know.

*

It's not the only   truth   I know.
That is the secret I hold
            in the pocket I keep
to myself.
In the pocket,
            my secret
is a crow,   my secret

is a small marble
you may have passed
a thousand times
        on the sidewalk,
and didn't even   know it.
You'd have stolen it   if you knew,
so even I wasn't allowed
                to know,
for I might have given it to you   freely.
I would have given my life
        freely, for my life was yours
when you broke me.

*

But look
        at my secret now,
                a small crow in my own pocket.
        Watch me preen, watch me chirp my little beak.
    Watch the me who grew   from all these spare
parts,   the me who hid,
the one who didn't believe
                I was   a piece of shit,
who didn't believe   I was an elevator
that went lower
                and lower until
                        I was in hell,

it felt like hell, but wasn't
because I was in my pocket.   I know
          it's confusing, but that's how it works,
because
               I'm sitting on the floor while I write this,
      and have a smile on my face
                              that I won't give away
for anything but a bullet,
               and even then I don't know
where it would travel,   but it wouldn't be far.
Look at it in the sky now,   Jon,
what came from breaking,
                              what's been built,
a whole city you could never imagine
          until you saw it with more than your eyes.
Please step
               back   and look
      at what grew,
what grows still
               even as it breaks
                              for the sky.

iii.

Timing is everything, Celia. Dreams have a ripeness just like fruit, and you can't let them rot on the tree.

— KAREN FINNEYFROCK

BEFORE THE BLOOM

One hundred fourteen days since last felt by touch.
Still alive, even that gentle, shy touch.

In order to hold, I'd have to reach—grab.
Love your smell in a room, won't even try touch.

Need a coat thicker than my body—
Like this whole city's a gone awry touch.

Calls move to voicemail, romance in poems.
All I feel is air, like my skin deny touch.

Woman in California, neck like an oasis:
keeps her heart in a box when she thinks of my touch.

Four miles this morning, sweat like baptism.
Take one deep breath, feel the whole sky touch.

Could spend my life pretending it's a long time.
Ripe for the pluck, either live or die touch.

LIVING ROOM MONOLOGUE
THE NIGHT OF WINTER FORMAL

January, 2001

From the outside, my house looks like most in Symmes Township. But *inside*, the first of three mix CDs I have made for this pre-party is rotating to slot one on a five-disc changer. To make a mix CD, you need to understand that you are casting a spell. Your subjects aren't allowed to know that you've broken into them with potions and flashlights, to reroute their chemistry for their own good. Folks think you can just tell people to have a good time. Bodies need to be romanced. I start with a quiet "Do Right Woman, Do Right Man," where Aretha Franklin is right up between your heart and ribs with a piano, organ, microphone, and this slow drummer. And your body sways like a blade of grass in the backwater swamp of your stomach; she just blows on it from the bottom and it hurts like the truth, like after this you could be ready for anything. The middle is crucial: what we inside my head like to call *Phase II*. The can't-miss song. "Kiss" by Prince, right? (Yes.) No! Something perfect, if thrown from nowhere, is not a song people know what to do with. You could find yourself at a party where people didn't even dance to Prince! Or worse, they know exactly what to do, it is gone too fast and nothing can follow. We are trying to make love all night here, people!

No Diggity.

From the start, it sneaks past your mind in all black, and talks only to your body. You don't even realize it came on. Look at you. You're just talking to whoever, but look again, whoever is smiling. You don't even hear Dr. Dre's first verse. You don't know he's in your lap, just little Dr. Dre, rapping, making beats, crawling up your arm to your neck to bring the drum in. Your train of thought left the station mid-sentence. The doctor is *in* with a drill in your vertebrae! You don't know your head was ever not bobbing. It's just you and this thing you used to think with, one buoy in the wide, wide ocean. When did you stand up? Where is your drink? Why are your hands in the air? You don't realize until it is too late that this is a team sport. Everyone in the song, the room, probably some folks driving by outside, in unison break into *Heyo heyo heyo hey yoo-ooo-ooo (that girl looks good) heyo heyo heyo hey yoo-ooo-ooo.*

Now play Prince. See what happens.

LOVE SPELL

I got close enough to your front door
to knock three times but I'm too busy
finishing my sandwich to knock.
Too busy transcribing the words

> to a D'Angelo song so I can sing it
> to you at a party that hasn't happened.
> I can feel the sky in its nightgown.
> The moon is a full turntable.

I don't want you to think I'm only writing
about cooking you dinner. I already
went to the grocery store.
They were out of crushed red pepper

> but I purchased four quarter-notes
> that I can fashion into a song.
> It's called a love ballad, and maybe
> you don't love me yet, but maybe

you do! My love-me-o-meter got broken
as a child. So what if you picked up
the phone and we went to the park,
and I said all the interesting thoughts

> I've accrued this month, and you
> told me one real story from childhood.
> Then I said this thing, I don't even
> think it's that great, just something

I would say. Of course that's what makes you
whisper, *Ahem, mic check 1, 4. Write a poem
next to me and ask which lines I prefer.*
I get quiet because your eyes are like marbles

      that glow at the bottom of a river.
      I can hear a ballad thirty leagues away.
      I don't mean to make it
      sound this magical.

80% of relationships
end in other relationships.
I don't mean to build the cart
before horses even live here

      but this is how my brain works;
      I'm a dreamboat; I'm a boat that carries
      dreams. I've sprung a leak
      and you look like a broomstick.

You look like the kind of storm
I might not need an umbrella for.
You look like day turned to dusk. Let's make a baby.
Wait! I meant, let's make a baseball!

      You got me.
      Hold my mind so I can't change it.
      Abracadabra.
      It's not magic. It's real.

WHEN I SEE ANDRE 3000
BUYING BANANAS AT TRADER JOE'S

I say, *Everything you've ever done*
has meant so much to me.
He says, *I've done PCP.*
I say, *That meant so much to me.*
He says, *I've lost my keys*
and took it out on a waitress.
I forgot to brush my teeth on Tuesday
and I do commercials for Gillette razors now.
I say, *I saw that commercial. So much to me.*

He is enjoying himself.
How about you, Tex? he says. And I can't
believe no one has ever called me Tex before!
I say, *Okay.*
I've been wearing the same undershirt
for a week-and-a-half.
I pose for every photograph.
I masturbated this morning
picturing a woman I made out with two years ago.
I am preachy and self-important
when I talk about race with my family.
Sometimes when I'm not listening
I make my face look like it's SUPER listening,
and I might be incapable of romantic love.

He says, *Did you hear my song*
about being incapable of romantic love?

I say, *It meant everything to me.*
He says, *This isn't working.*
I say, *Wait! I write poems? Would that help?*
He says, *I'm scared if you read one*
it might suck. I'm not ready to risk
having to say something.

I say,
What
if I
just
stare
at you?

We are walking now.
I say, *Say something*
only Andre 3000 would say.
He says, *I'm lonely.*
I say, *Oh my God.*
That was so brave.

I HAVE A BEER WITH A PROFESSOR
WHO DRINKS WITH HIS STUDENTS

He slurs his words like he had one in a thermos on the way,
and admits during the conversation on revision, *But what
the fuck do I know?* He's sweating through his linen shirt,
beads accumulate on his forehead, and this man's a genius.
His next meeting is with a classmate, and I was ten
when she was born, and I'm making this sound menacing
when all I want to say is that he's drunk, and what I want
to say more is how *not* uncomfortable I am. How little
I'm considering what's appropriate. Not only that, I kind of
like that he meets his students drunk. And I wasn't looking
to write this, but at the full-program party he did kiss
my classmate on the cheek in front of five other people, and
their embrace lasted longer than five seconds, and everyone
else got handshakes, and she is well into the back nine
of her 20s, so there's not a point where I can say anything but
that my drunk professor is meeting next with my 22-year-old
classmate, and it took me awhile, but I'm all in with him;
he makes my day better; he makes my writing better, and
here's where the thought enters my mind, and I can't make it
leave: when will I have to sit down with him? When will I
have to stop liking his Facebook posts, to carefully erase
his name when I talk about my mentors, to relay his wisdom
without giving him proper credit, to remove him from
the acknowledgment section of my book? And off of what?
That he was drunk in a bar with a student? That he kissed
a twenty-nine-year-old on the cheek at a party? I didn't
embrace anyone for five seconds at that party, but I was

drunk, and now I'm on the sidewalk because his next meeting
has started, and the one person I know in this neighborhood
is him, but I don't know him well enough to know
what's happening in there, probably just sound writing
advice, which is to say what I don't know is permission
enough to leave.

ODE TO THE RAT

after Samantha Thornhill

If we cleaned you up, you'd look like
a hamster. The little girl on the platform
would ask her mother if she could pet you.
Mom would say, *Of course.*
Brother to the pigeon,
creature of the city
where ooze is your bathtub.
God didn't make the sewers,
we did. So what
if there's piss and rainwater,
the rot of month-old milk
I poured down the drain
as if it were an eraser. Presto chango,
refrigerator clean.
Crystalized exhaust from our pipes
but you call it home.
You got a couch at the crib
made from a soda can.
You can learn a lot
by what a person throws away,
so you should have a seat at the U.N.:
Ambassador of the Trash Can.
Instead I come home late;
you run to greet me from under
a mound of plastic bags
filled with rotten apple cores
and empty cups of dried yogurt.

You scamper across my foot—
Me! who craves touch,
who would hold a stranger
on the subway if the mood were right.
I squeal, drop the groceries,
can't even look at you.
But now you're gone,
the moment seared into both of us.
I write this ode to you now,
but don't even think about coming inside.
I pick up the phone,
you're dead by the time I click *end*.
Deacon of disease,
sultan of the sewer,
envoy of the underbelly,
you get a box
that says *Poison*
but you can't read.

DANDELION

Two people face each other on a sidewalk
where below, Dandelion talks.
It's been sniffed at, stomped on, disheveled,
sees these two who didn't wish to see
each other. If either had known,
they'd have taken different avenues.
Dandelion absorbs the situation, has ears
in places you wouldn't think to look.
It came from a plant that came from a plant.
It has 400 babies due next week.
When you're only here for a moment,
Dandelion says, *any dispute looks petty.*
Dandelion sees the raven-colored cartridge emerge
ten times the size of a dandelion.
It watches the hand cock back,
each knuckle like the head of a baby bird.
A vein twitches along the man's right temple,
how beautiful he holds the cartridge, like a candle,
like it's safer to hold it than to bury himself
in a stack of blankets, safer than each step he could run
in the other direction. *Running is an option,*
says Dandelion, *but safety is not.*
The bullet has a twin bullet, a ghost bullet
that will travel backwards
into the eye of the shooter.
The shooter will see it plainly
when he looks in the mirror, will hide it
from his friends in conversation.

The Dandelion sees a full moon
once, maybe twice, in a lifetime.
There's no good moment, it says,
to be afraid. They don't hear it though.
Today is Dandelion's life's work.
It can make a robin's egg emerge
from the barrel. It knows it can.
It tries to morph into cool rain.
It focuses on the barrel, on the egg.
Birth, Dandelion says, *birth is what's important.*

ODE TO MY MOTHER'S HIP

My body remembers you from the inside—
the femurs parted like trombones in a backup band,
how she screamed with no choice but to accept.

We're on a bridge, and my mom has to put an arm
through my arm. She isn't the kind of person
who appreciates being over-asked if she's alright.
You're wrestling her to the concrete.
She hangs onto me more with each step,
less when she knows she's doing it.

The whole process is unnatural,
what they'll do to you.
Who opens a body to remove?
You've died, but she hasn't.
Stolen from the whole,
cast down the river,
but we are all soon
snuffed-out matches.
What could you possibly be, alone?
Dried calcium?

How far behind will the other parts be?
Her heart a leather sack, her body—
I, too, was a part
of her body,
then removed.

iv.

And everything under the sun is in tune
but the sun is eclipsed by the moon

—PINK FLOYD

THE TRICK WHEN SYNCHING *DARK SIDE* *OF THE MOON* WITH *THE WIZARD OF OZ*

October, 1998

I have to press play on the stereo at exactly the second roar of the MGM lion. It's not proven whether or not I have to be four-deep on a one-hitter, or if it has to be the night I learned how to make a White Russian only to crown myself *Lord Russian* or *Sir-Drinks-A-Lot*, or if I have to be 15 in the suburbs of Cincinnati with an understanding of what exactly there is to do around here. Getting fucked up is our Natural History Museum, our Modern Art Museum, and to a lesser extent our Public Library. Tonight we watch Dorothy scamper across the front yard amidst the incipient twister, as the album's voice says, *Why should I be frightened of dying? There's no reason for it.* Then Dorothy exits the farmhouse into a new world of color and munchkins and we are all exiting to the sound of cash registers like the one at LaRosa's Pizzeria where we all work and can be found some nights smoking L's behind the dumpster. I am trying to remember how I spent weekends only three years ago, before inspecting whose parents were out of town, or which basement could be jeopardized to the gods of discovery, or whose neighborhood held the most opportunity for creative vandalism (i.e., smashing someone's flower pots then ringing their doorbell; stealing tomatoes from a garden, carving them with a nail to throw them back at the same house then ringing their doorbell; taking turns defecating and peeing into a tennis ball can leaning said can against someone's front door then ringing their doorbell). Tonight, we are in Warner's parentless living room where two hours earlier Ox pretended he was going to hug Sarah but at the final moment twisted his body around to instead fart in her face, prompting all the girls to drive out into the pouring lightning storm and leave seven of us with only this invention of a movie where everything is happening for a reason. And as the final song of the album ends to the sound of our collected wonder,

something happens that can only happen in 1998.

The movie silently continues as the five-disc changer begins a loud rotation, only to land on Chumbawamba's "Tubthumping." The Wicked Witch of the West is on top of a barn pitching fire bombs at the scarecrow. Each time the scarecrow falls, and then scrambles to stand, the song says, *I get knocked down, but I get up again.* And we require no further evidence. The present is our religion. We are zealots, magnificent, hidden, explosive.

THE BASEMENT

September, 1997

When I was a freshman and no one was drunk, I had a crush on Anna Mason, and gave her a back massage in Ox's basement while we all watched *Groundhog Day*. My hands were draped across her bare back, and she was not leaving, which I took to mean that she was totally into it. I began to think that if she was this cool with my hands under the back of her shirt, how might she feel about the front of her shirt? Her newly minted b-cups were laid across my left thigh, and seemed to be humming "The Star Spangled Banner" to my two palms, like taking this chance was the kind of risky freedom this country was founded on. At the moment of truth, having never touched a boob in my fourteen-year life, I knew that when my fingertips slowly crept past her shoulder blade, either she would scream, *No!* Then I would spend an undetermined period of time attempting to live this down. Or,

when my fingers found the treasure she was subliminally guiding them toward, our bodies would experience a tacit euphoria, followed by something I wouldn't understand even if I knew how to name it. Would we kiss? Would I have to have sex? Would this make her my girlfriend? All I knew was boobs first. After three minutes of massaging her back and my ego, I made the unmistakable move. My left hand was still working into her back, but my right hand was now exclusively on the smooth surface of her right boob, and she did not move away, and a Fourth of July Parade erupted in my chest with sparklers and hot dogs and little kids with glitter red, white, and blue T-shirts that said *God Bless America* across the front.

We were plotting the impossible, and she was my co-conspirator: an immobile, electric green light I thought at any instant would explode into animation, I was just waiting for it to happen. Ox and Anna's two friends had left the room, which I thought seemed customary, and I could hear them just outside the door in what sounded like hushed laughter. I couldn't quite make out the words, but assumed it was simply the joy that stretched throughout any basement when two people were making magic. But then one word sang out from the river of whispers.

Asleep.

Anna and I had been sharing this experience. I had felt it, thus she must have also felt it. All the tiny narratives that had not occurred were crashing in from the ocean onto my parade. I hadn't kissed her. I hadn't asked her anything. I hadn't even looked in her eyes. I had known the moment sat on such a narrow ledge that I didn't want to give my chubby and stupid body the chance to ruin it.

I crawled my arm back out and up against my own chest. Anna sat up as the laughter from the hallway grew louder. We just sat there frozen for what must have only been seven seconds.

You know what just happened, right? I said.

Yeah, Anna said.

Okay, I said.

Then Anna got up and walked toward the laughter like it was a light. I sat alone in front of Bill Murray, who was carving an ice sculpture with a chainsaw. After three minutes Ox came into the room.

Anna is crying upstairs. She said you went up on her while she was asleep.

What? I said. *Dude, she wasn't asleep!*

I knew she wasn't asleep, and I clung to that knowledge like it was a hand attempting to save me from an express train I had just fallen out of. I could see four years extend like a driveway before me, could hear telephones ringing all over the school district, further and further from the epicenter of this basement. Monday was only two days away, and by the afternoon bell there wouldn't be one safe place for me.

I never meant for it to happen, but there it was.

I didn't want to know what I saw in Anna's eyes during those frozen seven seconds before the world changed. It wasn't sleep. It was fear.

I made it.

And I felt it too.

V.

I'm missing the six biggest screws
to hold this blessed mess together. I'm wind-
rattled. The wood's splitting. The hinges are
falling off. When the bridge ends,
just like that, I'm a flung open door.

—PATRICK ROSAL

V.

I SHOULD BE WRITING THE STORY

for Abe

I should be writing the story I'm working on
about the night I got suspended from high school,
but instead I'm browsing through photos on my computer
that lead to images of the night I turned twenty-one
and had to be carried up the front steps of my then-
ex-girlfriend's house. I threw up across her bedroom floor
and woke in her bed with the worst hangover I will ever have.
I'm looking for this picture from high school because
I am writing a story about the night I was suspended
for being drunk at my senior Winter Formal. But there you are
in a photo from Tennessee at that music festival where it rained
so hard I lost a Reebok to the mud. One yellow poncho
covers us both, except my head is what peaks out the top.
Newly in love, it was the poncho you got from Lindsey
when she studied at Michigan. That was the year your blood
clotted: your arm swelled to the size of a tree branch, and Jacob
had to speed you two and a half hours to Cincinnati.
You were sprawled in the backseat, a child trying not to die.
An ambulance then transported you four hours to Cleveland,
and I drove three hours to pick up your notes from college
because I was suspended from high school for being drunk
at a dance I was driven to by someone who was drunk
on Snider Road where you couldn't see the other cars
come over the hill, the same hill where I rode shotgun
next to you in the old Aerostar minivan where you'd gun it
and the digital speedometer topped at 85, and we'd hit the hill
and land at the bottom, right where someone's driveway let out,

and we'd laugh the whole way home about how people
were stupid if they didn't realize the fact you could do that
meant you were a great driver. I'm writing this story
about high school, and am not so stupid I can't see how
if a few rights went left you could have a gravestone
for a brother. I could have a shoebox of photos
I'm too afraid to look at in place of a bus ride to Boston
to hold two nephews who are becoming brothers,
whose arms around my legs I can no longer picture
who I'd be without.

AND IT WILL BE A BEAUTIFUL SONG

A woman sang on the Q84 today
as the bus landed your elbows

and shoulders into the intimate
space of people you didn't know.

She sang, *And it will be
a beautiful song* to the hair brushed

across her forehead like the fray
of a tablecloth, to the cane at her side.

Over and over. You told a classroom
about your heartsong today.

Said, *This week feels like sandbags
are on my heart, and most of me*

would like to know why. They said
this week is like that for everyone.

That our moods can be traced to humidity
or the turning of a season,

but it is the end of October
and will continually turn to Fall

until Winter. A sweet syrup crept
into her larynx as the bus listened.

Fifty people, but maybe it was just you.
You were carrying your heart

which is a kind of labor. Her song
knew the bus was not fooled

by the physical size of your bodies.
Your lives, a cup: the sloppy juice inside

continually rising until it spills.
The song will be a beautiful song,

and the bus, convinced
she is singing to each person

individually. This weight with them
always. You don't know the words

or each other, but have known
this song: the weight

of what you carry. It is okay
the rain made you cry.

A friend loses the woman who made him
and your first thought is to call your own mother.

A different empty waits in your bed
each morning. It only changes

but does not end. It will be
beautiful. It is okay. A trajectory.

A pull. A wake.

HEY MOM

for Kathy Sands

after Chance the Rapper

Monday morning, shower sing / like church
and then your phone rings / the room's blue
you see my name, it came through
wait let me buy a plane, I can't!
but let me buy a ticket
stop in Jersey for your sister Sue
and we'll just come and kick it
you on the couch while I make it cook
Mom, look at this / you made a book
I wrote the book / the cover's you
I'll paint your face / on volume two

I don't sing, but I wrote a song
even raised *your* mom to sing along
it could be the ringtone on your phone
not that you really care like that
just electric toys / you can take it back
but not me / won't trade your son
I won't trade thee / got no more moms
you got three / Abe and Ben and Jacob
but I'll put you on this boat with me
It flies though, now we're in space
split a chocolate stout like we split a face
look at me / I'm younger you
I got these eyes / you've got them blue
put a grandkid on it / she will too
you'll never crumble / no graves

a headstone on some enclave
your heart won't keep in one place

Your stories to my grandkids
we'll write your name in sparks
you'll probly want some water though
so I can be a shark / and you
can be my ocean / me I got this notion
you'll never understand this love I got
so me, I made this potion
It's part song / part postcard
part the times your heart scarred
part the times you lost love
part this bed / you rest up
part this world that's messed up
putting me right next to you
fuck this clock / time is blue
me and you / that's a crew

NEW YEARS

Nine drinks in at a party outside Cincinnati at a lake house
owned by four boys who were seniors when we were freshmen—
now we're seniors who don't know the fact they want us at
their party is proof they are less cool than we think they are—
it takes three boys to hold my body upside-down above the
keg with the spout just under my double chin while everyone
counts loud like rewinding a tape of the ball dropping. I land
on uneven pavement, throw a wink at Ox's silhouette. The
beat wobbles out of their club-sized speakers, and my knee
does this dip that if you froze it in a picture, might look like I
was praying. The alcohol burns out a space for me to sink into
the applause of the patio. Ninety minutes, I tumble onto the
concrete basement bathroom floor with the lights broken, and
almost fall asleep, but dignity forces a hand into my pocket to
procure two over-the-counter Yellow Jackets™ I bought from
Super America, the same pills that would make me throw up
radioactive-green on the senior cruise, but tonight they hit me
like a can of spinach, and it's not even midnight. I fling my coat
into the trunk of a red Jeep Cherokee I pray is Ox's, and make
it back to the patio without even a stumble. It's 11:45. Even the
thought of an impossible midnight kiss makes my waist grow
three inches and my brain become a hollow sphere someone
drained into the lake. I am years from dreaming anyone might
look at this ocean of suburban cool, and pick me. I throw my
hands toward the sky with enough dance moves to make the
party get wild. My eyelids are wide when I talk, and their faces
shine into all the rooms in me that have open shades. When

the ball drops on midnight, it is my boys I deserve, with whom I cry. We hold each other as our silent love grants a recess of permission to wash over the patio like a spilled bottle. I'm a big man. I have a big heart, and there is almost nothing I can't be.

ABOVE GROUND

I spent three weeks crafting a Facebook message to Anna
    with a 16-year-old apology
        for my 14-year-old self.
She wrote back, surprised at what she read,
    grateful, remembered:

when my hands first rounded her back,
    she'd been excited. Said I was funny,
that she'd liked me,   then she'd heard the laughter,
    knew I'd planned it, my friends, too,
        the world conspiring   always;
      that to be a "slut" was to be
in danger. So, she closed her eyes,
    said, *Asleep.*

I too felt the world conspiring. Felt fat, performative,
    on the verge of removal
        from any room I was proud to be in,
couldn't imagine that what she'd wanted
        was me.

    Because I couldn't imagine,
because to love myself wasn't yet
        on the table,
I didn't ask her for what I wanted.
    I risked, but not all of it,
not a hand offered to the empty air
      between us   where it could be held
    or rejected.

The lessons then:
    Don't ever do this again.
And, you were stupid to believe anyone
    would want you.

Do you, reader, understand what I'm saying?

    The small cruelties I delivered to myself
        rippled out like the surface of the water
after a stone's wound.
            I'm saying I see you out there, too, working.
    I see my own face in the crowd, now
        and at fourteen. I want to say to each of us
here in The Kingdom of Power Dynamics
    that you can't address the kingdom
        without addressing how you treat yourself.
That idea finally opened its eyes within me
        when Anna wrote back.

In New York, I fell in love with a woman who didn't love me,
    but I felt the words leave my chest
        aloud, and better than I could have imagined.
Later, on a bridge with a different woman,
            just before we kissed,
        my body quivered as I asked her
    if I could.
    Later still, I left my bathroom where I had stared
        at myself in the mirror for five minutes

like Eminem in *8 Mile*, to tell a new woman
      that knowing her sweetness
was the highlight of my year, and
              I wanted more.
    She replied that more was what she wanted
              to give.

Of course, before that, I was rejected
            in ways I might have predicted,
    but, look at what found us,
          fourteen-year-old Jon.
You were afraid then,
        as I am now,   of what they'd think of me.

Fear is what happens when I don't have an answer.
   I don't have
             an answer,
      but the future is built
on the words I release
        into the air.

THE SHORELINE

I threw my hands from my wrists because I liked
the way the beat sniffed around the speakers
like a dog searching for the right place to shit.
My butt was against my blue jeans
against the ripped leather of some couch listening
to some beautiful poet profess what they dreamt about once,
because we are scared to write out the new dreams,
because they are happening *right now*,
which is a good time to tell you that I am not alone.
I'm next to one hot cup of soup. She could melt the wax
off the wick if you catch my baseball. I don't
know her. Just two people, one couch,
and a bundle of old dreams, but I cross my left leg
in her direction like a knight
if the couch were a chess board.

In my newest dream, I think I see her see me. I think
I see her adjust her butt against her pants against the leather
right now, which is a good time to tell you
that my heart has not been working right.
It's a cold bowl of wax. It could freeze the juice
off a mango. I have been carrying
this pistachio in my ribs for months.
I have been trusting people only when I write about them.
I have been straight-to-voicemail. I have been sewing
a dress from all of these books and wearing it
to my one-man prom. I don't know
what her hair smells like, but I want to.

I don't know what her mother's name is,
but I want to send her an email questionnaire.
I want to reach my arm to the right, now,
which is a good time to tell you that she
is actually two ladies—

 one I got an email from that said
she'd only met me but she knew me;
she only knew me but she loved me.
I said, *I don't believe in magic outside of my poems.*
I said, *You can't love me, all I did was write a book,*
and she still wrote back. One I liked
the comment she made on someone else's Facebook status,
and it isn't the one right here, but my elbows
heard the beat ride out the speakers on horseback.
My shoulders got yanked by some invisible lasso.
I am talking to the air with my entire body,

and if I was waiting for the perfect time
to say *HowDoYouDo?*
For an invitation to a dinner party;
for a flow chart to say *Trust is a risk
like poetry*; for a sign to spark
in the back of all these old dreams that said,
Jon, let it ride . . .

I am already thirty, old enough
to know one day my heart will shut down
altogether. I get to choose for what.

THE DAY WE CHOSE INSTEAD TO GROW

Maggie met me for coffee at 9 a.m.,
our relationship so new we weren't
even calling it that. It didn't make sense
that I would leave; she was honey at the end
of whatever road turned me out, left for dead,
a path that now called me backwards, demanded
I re-join the shadow that had grown over my heart.
I was 14 when dad left for those weeks,
years before anyone could talk about it.
Mom,
the way you looked down at the pavement
on our walk, unable to dress up the pain,
the fear you were now a broken woman,
the way you tried to comfort me, but instead cried,
and I did nothing to help, which made me worse than dad,
I kept that image in my brain for years, where it simmered.
Here it was over coffee, telling me I had to leave,
to re-join the art project I'd made from emptiness.
Maggie could've slapped me and been justified,
could've brought up the gates, sunk into her own rot.
She rubbed my hand; she bought me breakfast,
put two lips on my neck and told me it seemed hard,
that maybe I could explain it later when it was less difficult.
That was the day the Bengals lost in the playoffs,
and Daniel died, and I couldn't move on my bed
while she packed my lunch for a reading at a high school
with a friend I'd already lost. It's a lot to even write it.

I remember her taking off my jeans, sliding on my sweatpants.
I remember the two sandwiches I watched her make.
I remember how she kissed my forehead
the way you might have when I was young.
I remember knowing I didn't need another mother,
but seeing through the fog how lucky I was
to know her. How she chose to keep me.
How facing an old headwind, I chose it too.
How small I was then.

ACKNOWLEDGMENTS

Thank you so much to the following journals, which published poems in this collection, sometimes in previous versions: *Hanging Loose, Muzzle, Lumina, Good Weather for Media, Word Riot, The Rattling Wall from PEN Center USA, Rattle, Uncommon Core, Thrush, No Dear, The Nervous Breakdown, phati'tude, Learn Then Burn: Volume 2.*

"Decoded" was reprinted in *Best American Poetry 2014.*

NOTES

The quote in the fifth stanza of "Decoded" is from Barack Obama, March, 2012.

The title "I Know That Silence Will Greet Me . . ." is from the Wislawa Szymborska poem "Pursuit."

"To My Ohio, a Letter Home" was written partly in conjunction with Peter Schumann's exhibit *The Shatterer*, at the Queens Museum. In that exhibit, he repurposed, as I have, J. Robert Oppenheimer's famous quote from the Bhagavad-Gita, "Now I am become Death, the destroyer of worlds."

The song "No Diggity" is by Blackstreet, featuring Dr. Dre and Queen Pen.

The album *Dark Side of the Moon* is by Pink Floyd.

The title "The Shoreline" is partially inspired by the first line of Audre Lorde's poem "A Litany for Survival."

In "The Shoreline," the phrase "*let it ride*" is an allusion to a line from Jack McCarthy in his poem "The Spaces Between."

The quote from Anis Mojgani is from the poem "The Giant Golden Boy of Biology," which appears in the poetry collection *The Feather Room*.

The quote from Ada Limón is from the poem "The Quiet Machine," which appears in the poetry collection *Bright Dead Things*.

The quote from Karen Finneyfrock is from the novel *The Sweet Revenge of Celia Door.*

The quote from Pink Floyd is from the song "Eclipse," which appears on the album *Dark Side of the Moon.*

The quote from Patrick Rosal is from the poem "Brokeheart: Just Like That," which appears in the poetry collection *Brooklyn Antediluvian.*

THANK YOU

I am unbelievably grateful both for and to my parents, Kathy and Josh Sands. There is no me, no book, no magic, no patience, no growth, no nothing without you, and the well of knowledge and love that you've gifted me.

To my Sands family: Jacob, Abe, Ben, Chad, Lindsey, Wendell, Janet, Emma, Eli, Isaac, and Olivia, you've done me a great service in permitting me to tell some of our stories. I don't take it for granted. I love each of you, individually, collectively, and always.

To my unparalleled editors, my forever first eyes: Jeanann Verlee, Adam Falkner, Lauren Whitehead, and Maggie Ambrosino-Sands, this book exists because of you. Thank you for your expansive vision, your compassionate honesty, and your genius brains.

I can't begin to explain how thankful I am for the community of writers and friends who push and support me, so many people I'm proud to live and write alongside. I could never list you all here, but let me just say: Jeanann Verlee, Adam Falkner, Lauren Whitehead, Carlos Andrés Gómez, Mahogany L. Browne, Phil Kaye, José Olivarez, Aziza Barnes, Eboni Hogan, Jive Poetic, Derrick C. Brown, Sofía Snow, Ken Arkind, Samantha Thornhill, Reed Swier, Geoff Kagan-Trenchard, Emily Kagan-Trenchard, Rico Frederick, Roya Marsh, Anis Mojgani, Elana Bell, Jai Chakrabarti, Josh MacPhee, Noel Quiñones, Ashley August, Joel Francois, Timothy DuWhite, Sean DesVignes, Nathalie Thille, Aracelis Girmay, Willie Perdomo, and Patricia

Smith, I see your influence and example throughout this book, throughout my life.

To my Ambrosino family: Nancy, Drake, Burger, Ashley, Cara, Brad, Joel, Betsy, Coert, Jordan, Max, Char, Gus, Isaac, Beatrice, and Sloan, I don't know how I ever got lucky enough to have a second family. My heart is yours.

To Ox and Warner, whose love and friendship are priceless. To Prince, Fish, Gulker, Knowledge, Brisben, Scherch, Cory, and Zack, whose big hearts I'm grateful to have lived alongside.

To Joshua Henkin, Dinaw Mengestu, Julie Orringer, Sigrid Nunez, Ellen Tremper, Meera Nair, Ernesto Mestre, Geoffrey Minter, and the Brooklyn College MFA in Fiction, thank you for expanding my lens, for teaching me how many different ways there are to be precise.

To Urban Word NYC, Bailey House, Write Bloody Publishing, SupaDupaFresh, Brooklyn College, the Adirondack Center for Writing, Lincoln Center Education, the Interference Archive, the LouderARTS Project, and each organization that has supported my work as a writer and educator, thank you a million times over.

To Harriet Barlow, Ben Strader, and the staff at the Blue Mountain Center, many of these poems were written under the care of your unmatched hospitality.

To Jeanne Kabenji, you are a true light, and I'm forever grateful to know you.

To all of my students, you've taught me more than I can quantify.

To Beth Dial and the National Poetry Series, for the tradition you've created and maintained.

To Helene Atwan and the staff at Beacon Press, for believing in this book, and for all that you do.

To Richard Blanco, I can't thank you enough for giving these poems, each with such quiet beginnings, a place to rest.

To Mish, the sweetest young man in the whole wide world.

To Maggie, I look at each of these stories, and I think of them leading to you. You've changed my life forever. My great love.

JON SANDS is the author of *The New Clean*, published in 2011. His work has been featured in the *New York Times* and anthologized in *The Best American Poetry*. Sands has received residencies and fellowships from the Blue Mountain Center, the Brooklyn Arts Council, the Council of Literary Magazines and Presses, and the Jerome Foundation. He is a facilitator with the Dialogue Arts Project and the cohost of *The Poetry Gods* podcast. He teaches weekly writing workshops for adults at Bailey House in East Harlem. Though he tours extensively as a poet, he lives in Brooklyn, New York.

RICHARD BLANCO, who served as President Obama's inaugural poet in 2013, is the author of two memoirs and five volumes of poetry, the most recent being *How to Love a Country*. He currently serves as the Education Ambassador for the American Academy of Poets.